Breather

BREATHER

poems by Ioanna Carlsen

OFF THE GRID PRESS

Off the Grid Press is an imprint of Grid Books.

www.grid-books.org

Acknowledgments:
Agni: "Giacometti, Nine Figures," "A Poem Called Baroque"
Alaska Quarterly Review: "Road Trip," "Eighteenth Century Japanese Screen, Kyoto"
Beloit Poetry Journal: "Insomnia"
Cerise Press: "A Doll's House," "Breather I"
Earthships: "Eighteenth Century Japanese Screen"
Ginkgo Tree Review: "Underwater Room"
Glimmer Train: "Horse-Washing Waterfall, Hokusai"
Kit-Kat Review: "Arrival"
The New Guard: "Two Variations on a Borrowed Phrase"
Nimrod: "Small Husband and Wife Series with Gods"

Cover illustration: Franz Ludwig Catel, *A View of Naples through a Window*, 1824 (detail). Reproduced courtesy of the Cleveland Museum of Art.

Printed on acid-free paper by Cushing-Malloy, Inc. Ann Arbor, Michigan.
Book design by Michael Alpert.

ISBN: 978-1-946830-04-3

This book is for my mother.

CONTENTS

I. Paris Air

Duchamp's Paris Air (50 cc of Paris Air)

of December 1919, consists of a chemist's ampoule

emptied of its fluid and labeled "Serum physiologique,"

which Duchamp had brought back from Paris for Walter

Arensberg, "who had everything money could buy. So I

brought him back an ampoule of Paris air."

"Art is a container for emptiness, or an empty container holding nothing."

– Marcel Duchamp

"But what is it to be at home, Mr. Tyler, what is it to be at home?
A lingering dissolution."

– Samuel Beckett

Two Variations on a Borrowed Phrase

"...how neatly silence describes the thing"
    – Jorie Graham

I. Home

Knowing the place so well it's always a surprise,
returning,
to notice something you had not remembered,
how much work you must have done on the garden,
or something you had forgotten,
a painting someone did when they were ten,
and that old emptiness in the hallway
amid the familiar, the known, the lived-with,
the frequently handled—and
the sooner-or-later-to-be-permanently-left,
the-not-to-be-returned-to.

The dog sniffs something new,
perhaps the strange scent of the sea on you,
and as you unload your luggage,
a tunneling of pain reminds you
how long you have been roaming the earth,
mostly in these rooms,
and this manifests
as a slight apprehension when taking messages
off the machine:
returning to the ordinary, it seems fraught with danger,
extra-ordinary, or more beautiful than you had thought,
and you more lucky to be here,
because instead of living it
you *know* you're living it:
the glinting, wordy, bobbing lake of the day,
the lap of night.

And how does the returned-to receive you?
Like a dog who cannot be told when,
(Wednesday, June 28th, means nothing to a dog)
if ever, you are coming back—
absence just happens to a dog,
and the house and all its objects, the fireplace,
your favorite chair, the green vase on the sill,
the clock,
did not even know you were gone,
how neatly silence describes the thing,
your return.

II. Pleasure

I'm curious about pleasure,
is it a sensation or an emotion
and what is the difference, I mean
what is a feeling, how do you touch it,
how are you touched by one, I'm curious
about how your emotions fit you like what you wear,
sadness a glove you can remove by drinking or shopping,
depression, a dress too tight to get off,
the blouse of laughter—
and where do they all go,
the pleasure you took,
the sadness you felt,
where do they go when they go?

I hope the diver who eventually dredges this corner of the bay
brings up trunks full of dubloons, and the letters
of rapscallions,
and things
of things, artifacts belonging to the dead,
and I hope that ship is sunk deep in the water as a fish,
and that the diver as he retrieves
the belongings of breathers dressed in silence
thinks of pleasure down there in the deeps,
how when sensation sleeps, the world turns into a dot
from which you can see forever,
how you fall asleep saying nothing,
wake to a big dream.

Woman at Home

She likes to have the evening come over her
without the lights on—that's when she sees things:
the lights turning on outside automatically, insomnia
entering the house.
She sits with the lights off, it's like going blind.

Then pure sound comes on,
crickets haze the space around her,
the afghan silts into valleys
and what's outside is the same as what's in—
the room is inside-out,

part of the earth, a grave
she still has hearing inside of.
Before she even knows it,
darkness invests the room,
and the windows frame what's left:

ragged blue fragments,
out back, barking,
heat and a wind coming in,
the windows full of accident,
the world looking in, watching.

Herself nothing but a dream inside the world's head.

objets trouvés:

"I thought I might be happier after dinner, but I have had dinner."
                                                    – Florine Stetthiemer

"From contact with the French, one learns to be unhappy politely."
                                                                – Cioran

Insomnia: A Sextet

I. On Reading Cioran

Leaf caught in a branch of ice,
I am unsleeping,
heroic,
neither dead, nor dreaming,
awake.

I exist when I
don't sleep,
it makes me feel
you there,
me watched.

You think because you
are not God
I don't know you.

But I've been here as long as you,
I know the territory:
(it's yours and mine)
our marriage is
the first map.

II. The Insomnia of Galaxies

is archipelagos
not knowing where they end,
but swirling by each other endlessly,
sleepless

a sea of one accident succeeding another,
moons circling moons,
breath succeeding breath,

sleep, you, sleep, in stillness rest.

III. Virtual Insomnia

Sleepless,
a picture of Giacometti's
Woman Standing stands on the sill,
next to dead roses and a clock.
On a chair, a book propped open, wide awake,
shows a woman Utamaro drew once.
Absent-minded,
she sticks a toothpick
through closed lips.

Outside it snows—
who is "it"?
In another room
the weatherman
thinks he knows what whoever is snowing
is going to do with it.
A series of "it"s
underlines the truth—
he doesn't know who snows either,
but streaks the early morning with a stream of empty sound.

IV. Virtual Sleep

In the air over the lake
the big birds fly, wheeling;
they scissor the light,
pattern over pattern, invisible scribbling,
and later,
dive into the trees
for truth.

V. Actual Sleep

The world was smothering me;
I took its hand off my mouth,
it was remarkably easy,
a little pressure on the wrist
and it lifted,
I dreamed in a different direction.
(I became the world
and it turned out to be nothing
but possibilities to contain me.)

VI. The Marriage of Sleep and Insomnia

I think of people missing from my life
as gone
but not yet returning.
Or returning
but not yet returned.
Either
is equal
in the eyes of my life.

When I think of you
with my eyes closed
I wonder
if tonight is one of those times
when you are here or not.
Actually come back.
Virtually tell me.

Show me in dreams
what I already know:
we have borne between us this marriage,
our conversations a beast with two backs.

Embers

You're breathing like a stevedore,
carrying something very heavy up a steep slope,
your right arm sticks up
out of the covers against the pillow
like the neck of a ghost—
I am quite at home in this atmosphere,
waiting for something to return
while you sleep, your sleep slipping,
seeping, into a world of snores.

That something which returns,
where has it been, and is it you?
Pascal tried to think it out—
what is matter, where is the soul,
what part of us feels pleasure—
is it our arm, is it our hand,
is it our flesh, our blood?
No, he decided. It was, he said,
something immaterial.

There, in the immaterial,
(which must be a place like any other)
as a snore is in a sleep,
(wherever either of those is),
in just those kinds of places—
in the sleeve of a coat
where Pascal hid the proof
(which no one can quite locate)
that God exists—

time seems to focus
its intricate desires,
and indicates
that *because* they exist,

therefore also
something nebulous exists
which will one day take us,
if not to God, at least
as far as the stars—

your sleep, between snores,
is like a death I wake to:
my own living,
the fire still burning,
and I see in there—
and who can prove otherwise—
a lady in the embers
who has a towering headdress,
flames like feathers.

I make no claims for her return
as she topples head over dress,
heels into ash.
Where she travels nobody knows,
the world is a road.

Pascal is reasonable,
pretends to nothing more
than he feels he can believe—
tethers his question
to the mysterious in its answer:
what feels is not flesh,
what *feels* is what
has traveled into being.

According to him,
to arrive here *once* is a miracle.
And I believe him, breather,
don't you?

Readymade: With Hidden Noise

"When I come here, to New York, it's with the idea of resting.
Resting up for nothing, since one is always tired,
even of existing."

"I like living, breathing better than working. . . .
Each second, each breath is a work which is inscribed
nowhere . . .
it's a kind of constant euphoria."

"I always asked myself *why* a lot, and from that questioning came doubt,
doubt of everything. I came to doubt so much that in 1923 I said,
Good, that's going well."

"In advance of the Broken Arm
 . . . was a snow shovel.
In fact, I had written that phrase on it.
Obviously I was hoping it was without sense,
but deep down everything ends up by having some."

"One changes.
One accepts everything,
while laughing just the same.
You don't have to give in too much.
You accept to please other people, more than yourself.
It's a sort of politeness . . . "

"Almost every evening before retiring. . . . Mme Duchamp and her husband
    were in the habit of reading funny stories aloud to each other.
the joke would leave both of them laughing just before going to bed.
On the evening of Oct. 2, 1968, it was his turn to read and, as usual, when
    the punch line came,
they both laughed exuberantly.
But on this particular evening,
while laughing,
Duchamp quietly closed his eyes and expired."

II. Infra-thin

"The space between

the front and back

of a sheet of

paper is an

example

of infra-thin."

". . . the touch of

a shadow

on an object . . ."

– Marcel Duchamp

Readymade: Traveller's Folding Item

". . . visible creation
is the terminus or circumference
of the invisible world."

"Giacometti's figures kept on shrinking,
as if by a will
to become the least common denominator
of the visible."

The Sahara: "Silence is a sound here."

The Peaches Are Coming Ripe, There's No Stopping Them

"The air is full of our cries."
— Samuel Beckett

The statue hasn't moved
since you lugged it from the truck
up the walk
to its position overlooking the garden
from the terrace—
a boy on a dolphin,
like a turret.

Your heart's blood gives up its wish to live forever
and hemorrhages over the thought
of autumn,
which keeps on coming, taking over
everything,
like an aging parent whose life
eclipses yours.

The peaches are coming ripe,
and if they remind you
of yourself, it's only
because you think
you are losing everything,
when in fact, you believe,
no matter how much the world changes,
no matter how insubstantial matter is,
your existence in the flesh
is constant as a cricket's chirping

and you wonder,
thinking of yourself,
who could kill such
a constant thing,

who could turn away from such insistence,
who could ever leave it
dying on its back?

But this is a noisy world
and what you choose to save
depends on how well you listen
and who you listen to.
There are other voices besides the busy crickets'
and they cry also
before fading infra-thin into the dark.

Giacometti, Nine Figures

after any arrival
existence
takes shape
and then the vanishing
takes place,
simultaneously
minutes slope
into the forgotten
sand in an hourglass,
shifting and granulated

the men stride,
caught in the act,

the women wait like death

seeing is forgetting the name
of what is seen, is *being* the thing
one sees.

He used to eat at midnight,
then work some more,
this thing that is reality, an obsession,
to find a way into it,
and a way out

thinness,
distillate of experience
diminishment of density,
elongation the solution,

substance dissolving into spirit

one more thrust of his thumb,
one more knick of his knife,
the figure crumbles,

the gaze has dignity,
but death is everywhere

his mother's skirt,
touching the ground,
terrifying
like pears in a painting
that will not stay put

Who Do You Think You Are?

Three-quarter moon,
shape of these young peaches back-lit by sun,
green, but with an aureole.
In this imperfect world
correspondences are not easy—
you glimpse the elusive and demean it
to fit visible sizes and forms.

Enemies come in seven doors, and go out one,
salvage what you can:
on your page this sliver of a caterpillar,
glimmering orange in the light,
turning grey when it reaches the shadows
could be a vision (if you knew that language)
of the world to come.

If only you could believe
this peach right in front of you—
actually the size and shape of the moon,
the way you materially see it—

if only you could believe this
is an idea you are capable of
because God had it first.
Those who live in God's world,
outside God's word,
tremble at the rustling of a leaf—
so, who do you think you are
breathing in such a wind—
the moon like food,
ideas ripening like peaches?

A Poem Called Baroque

After *Baroques* by Giovanni Careri,
with photography by Ferrante Ferranti

Even the photographer's name
(you wonder if he made it up)
is your first introduction
to a major symptom that constitutes
the baroque:
the drama of repetition, a nervous neurosis
it never tires of displaying.

Every page turned
leads to another histrionic image
the baroque stuffs itself with—
fat cupids, urns, acanthus, a rooster,
gargoyles peering off cathedrals
into an abyss,
the halo around death.

Abduction, rape, and murder
are the forms used,
romance tailored to the jugular,
every image so ready to die for love.
Seizure of another's body,
are the particulars—
hands clawed, beautifully, over a thigh,

resulting in
the stupefaction of the captured,
after the hysterical attempt of the victim
to flee the event,
which is then turned into the beautiful,
a tree, a map of Europe, the world
after death.

The interest the trapped
carry for you, the watchers,
mounts to a fascination
with those looked at
by what they can't see,
like statues or the dead:
defense and escape impossible,

the kneeling of life before chaos,
a constant *pietà*.

Twilight

For my mother.

I.

> "Figment dawn dispeller of figments
> and the other called dusk."
> – Samuel Beckett

That particular blue,
the infra-thin
of regret,

by which I still
so much know you.

Elongated
as a fourth dimension.

The darker it gets
the harder I fall
for all the traps I
set for myself
to keep me with you—

you were always so much
more innocent than
I thought.

II.

A blue that slips
out of a lighter color
and then sinks
into the trees,
taking secrets with it—

your dresses, your perfume,
what I have left,
the love we never
quite showed each other,
the reasons why we couldn't,
all blue too,
pride goeth before,
dusk follows.

III. The Fourth Dimension

"The fourth dimension became a thing you talked about,
without knowing what it meant. In fact, it is still done."

"Art is an outlet toward regions
which are not ruled by space and time."

– Marcel Duchamp

"In the background of *The Bride*, Duchamp once said, he had caught
a glimpse, for the first time, of the fourth dimension. This suggests
that he saw his Munich bride as a three-dimensional projection
of an invisible four-dimensional being."

– Calvin Tomkins, in a biography of Duchamp

Readymade: A Country Road. A Tree. Evening.

"It's always evening in Beckett, and always an interminable one."

"Nothing happens, twice."

"You may find nothing in it, and yet never forget it."

"What are you writing at the moment? Another blot on silence."

"Endgame is a constant preparation for leave-taking, the story of two men
who want to leave, but who also never arrive."

"Parting is always incomplete: at close of play Clov, the only character who
can move, remains motionless, frozen in a brief stage tableau that lasts
forever."

"The will has been opened, the unnamable utters, nothing for anybody."

"My life, my life, now I speak of it as something over, now as a joke which
still goes on, and it is neither—for at the same time it is over, and it goes
on, and is there any tense for that?"

"The self conceived as a place—as a non-dimensional place, outside of space
and time."

"Tympanum: on the one side the outside and on the other the in,
thin as foil,
two surfaces and no thickness,
perhaps that's what I feel,
myself vibrating,
on one hand the mind on the other the world I don't belong to either."

"To reach this timeless empty sphere that is his universe, Murphy makes
a downward journey through the three zones of his mind towards a
bottommost point where he is not free, but

a mote in the dark
of absolute
freedom."

Road Trip

I've always wanted to paint
the way the road eats up your life,
the way you drive right into it

how at night the street signs catching your lights
take on the mood of the music on the radio tilting sadly to the right—
how even during the morning the soft whir of the car
brings you so close to sleep
you can see the wheat in the fields
through your eyelids,

how late in the afternoon
over small poolings of water reflecting trees against the sky,
birds fly through birds,
one flock through another—
wings almost touching wings
in spite of so much space around them—

how barns were called hip-roofed,
how words exist in time like anything else
and fly through other words,
their wingtips brushing other wings,
how some sleep now
under the fields behind closed eyelids

how tonight, after the substructure of the rural,
we look forward, toward
the hard edges of the city

how it all passes,
how all the things you dread
shall come to pass,
and also pass,

wings whirring by wings
and the idea of infinity.

Phillip Glass

Tell me,
tell me again and again,
make only small changes.
But when you change, make sure I'm surprised,
make sure it's like undertow,
that leaves me roiling,
myself rolling over and down
into land's end, water everywhere,
overhead and to hand,

show me death—
compose submerging
(show me that was the world,
the most I could ever know)—

monotony is ritual,
same is soothing,
repetition primitive, reassuring—
it makes sure I know what you know,
keeps it simple, minimal:
that which you know,
that which you heard, that
which you have seen,
that *what* which you are,

show me life—
compose submerging,
show me this is the world,
the most I can ever know

both landscape and set dissolving with the last note.

Eighteenth Century Japanese Screen

Sometimes, later in the evening,
I think I see the figures move,

little people walking
through the dirt streets of a village
dressed in black or light blue,

leading an occasional white horse

the town
dressed in the light of the passed
wearing another dimension.

A lake inhabits the second panel,

a town the first,
a park the third,
I cannot see the fourth,

it is hidden by a wall of the present.

Occasional though they are,
why are all the horses white you might ask:
string theory I answer—

with eleven more dimensions

the unusual could be normal,
the normal stranger—
the peaked roofs of the houses,

the globular trees, imperfect lakes,

the temples like mountains,
could be one bridge after another,

leading out of this world.

Everything here is imaginary
or dead—the planes inside the picture
could contain both,

while pretending to be neither—

cranes, swans, and egrets,
origami designs in the landscape,
which appear to be
perpetually getting away
in the gold, gilded background
that must be autumn.

We live only in one dimension

such is luck, human,
to look at a picture and hear sadness
cry like a duck flying over a lake

that has fallen asleep
in a twilight that visits forever.

A Meditation on the Meditations of Descartes

He thought of himself "as having a face, hands, arms . . . this mech-
anism composed of bone and flesh and members, just as it appears
in a corpse, and which . . . [he] designated by the name of 'body.'"

In the name of the body
I watch the moonlight
and think upon waking in the middle of the night
that it is snow—

nothing is so certain as the fact that it looks like snow
but *is not*, it has not the substance,
has not the body of frozen particles,
but *is,* only a shining.
And nothing is so uncertain as the truth
in the words by which I designate the certainty
that snow is frozen light
that melts tomorrow when the sun sees it.

Further down the length of the lawn,
what I see in the eye of my mind
is a mute traveler,
coming from somewhere somehow far—
the shadow of his light, "rarefied and subtle as a soul,"
touching the body of this world:
I bathe in the stream of his light,
certain of nothing but the swiftness of his voyage
through the body of this house,
rifling drawers,
stealing across tiles
and then thresholds,

where he becomes snow,
particles of light frozen into a word.

Underwater Room

It's the way the ceiling floats all hung with shadows and light,
gleamings, promises.
It's things outside doing things:
leaves and branches, trees.
Glimmering is one thing,
(riddled shade,
nothing touching nothing),
noise is another—
you know the wind,
you know the wind soughing
against the house,
you know if you were
ashes, it would be your dust.

And if you could be dust,
you know you would float,
wisp and thread yourself through
doorways and screens—
you are the gleam in the pane mixed up in the trees outside,
you are life seen through glass,
serious silence,
the last word.

IV. Nobody's Perfect

Alfred Barr challenged Duchamp's insistence that he had selected each readymade on the basis of visual indifference.

'But, oh, Marcel,' Barr said, 'why do they look so beautiful today?'

Duchamp: "Nobody's perfect."

Readymade: Why Not Sneeze?

To be an artist is to fail.
The problem: defining the undefinable, naming the unnamable.
The problem of pinpointing a timeless center with a temporal and spatial
    pin. The problem: pursuing an infinitely receding something which . . .
has the characteristics of nothing.

I don't know if I work in order to do something
or in order to know why I can't do what I want to do.

You want art, you want the thing too, ok, I fix.

Husband and Wife Series with Gods

I. After Reading Calasso's *Literature and the Gods*

"What is a god?
Or where are the gods,
or how do you see them,"
he asked,
and so I answered,
"that lilac right there, its blooming,
that is a god,
and spring is a god,
the three graces, as in Boticelli—
the three graces are spring manifested
in a painting, the benediction of it,
the grace of the earth, its gifts,
and that moon by day up there
behind your back,
that is a god
and he is rolling his one eye at you,
and thinks, that little man
down there weeding his garden,
how stupid, should I trample him
as I would grasses,
and should I do it now, or
hold off till later," I said,
and he replied,
well that last is not a very interesting thought,
that is a cliché,
and I said, yes, but trampling
is one of the things gods do,
and their coming is often terrible,
like that of a husband.

II. Spring

What could I say that would not jar the pristine
(such a white place) nature of his perceptions?
The little curlicues of the lime-yellow forsythia
advise me to be quiet,
for trouble lurks to the left of any statement I might make,
but freedom to say whatever I like springs to the right.

How delicate the season, I could for example say,
which is what he brought me out to see;
but that might not be an acceptable phrase,
and besides, I made the mistake of talking about gods,

spring is a god, I said,
and from there digressed to ideas <u>about</u> gods,
finally reaching necessity
by way of accident.

Stop talking and look at it, he essentially said,
and I did—later, after our little fight.
Of course, as ever, he is right:
he's not just shutting up a wife,
but, as always, is thinking of both our interests—
the way I look is to write.

III. Paradiso

In this world
paradise comes before Inferno, not after—
it's what we have,
it's what there is.

I watch the birds flit by, visiting the fountain,
and you in disguise as a gardener, divorced from me—
out there—
while I am here on the terrace,
just an observer, not your wife.

Your red Hawaiian shirt, appearing, intermittently,
behind the lilac and the mulberry
reminds me I actually know you:
I was with you (behind the shrubbery) when you bought it,
its white flowers blossom now in the light—

inside the many greens of the leaves,
light promises revelation,
and keeps its word—

I have that feeling of being dipped in life,
all my body so preciously saved except where some nymph held me
by the heel,

and there, only in that place, is where necessity
and change slip through—and I find, like the wasps do,
(just on the other side of a miniscule crack behind the stone wall)
the huge tunnel the mole made.

Gardening, you move closer, into the foreground,
your nose shines, highlighted,
your glasses glaze white, the flowers blaze light—

and already in the glare I see the snake
approaching, the apple so desirable in its completeness,
already I know the fall that will come of these last years of marriage

and if I am first,
like a good wife,
I will endure it, and not complain,
and how unhappy at last you will be
when finally I refuse
(I'm sure that's how you will then see it)
to say a word.

Ballerina

Back in that world
where the dog growls like a stomach,
involuntary, bestial, forgiven,
where a leg appears in a child's drawing
as part of a cross, a face
imposed in its upper limits,
quizzical and a little mad,
exposing a logic we cannot claim to understand,
but love,

back there,
where no resistance occurs,
the dream appears on which we stake
what we are.

From that world Balanchine
(who married ballerinas)
comments on a scene
from one of his ballets—
a parallelogram of four arms
poised above four toe shoes—
by saying, with a deep shrug,
"How much story do you want?"—

as if the story
were only the cause,
which it is,

a symptom,
only emblematic of its form,
which it is.

Nine Standing Figures, Giacometti

I.

with pedestals like cattle cars
they're incandescent
gas-ovened,
cradle to grave
mummy-shaped

II.

flat, thin figures
braced to receive what happens
joy not part of it

III.

they exist,
almost human

too thin to live,
too thick to die

IV.

tall figures:

they turn the real into that
gesture,
an urn with legs

V.

creatures ribboned
into metallically hammered-out space,

however whittled away
they know something

VI.

objects transformed into subjects,

subjects returning to objects

strangers will love

V. Absence

"His hair, his face, his hands, his clothes
were so penetrated with plaster dust that
no amount of washing or brushing could
eliminate it, and the streets neighboring
the *Hotel de Rive* bore the ghostly
imprints of his footsteps."

– James Lord, biographer
of Alberto Giacometti

I Wanted to Fall

I wanted to fall as far as I could,
and not see where it got me—
when you finally want to fall
you want to fall
with the luck of no return,
as far as you can—
it's an art, it takes art,
sometimes you have to prepare for it.
Other times
for no reason
sirens sing, *the wet path opens*,
and off you go,
tumbling into water
with a voice in it,
plumbing the length you have to travel
with a noise like raining,
verbs of water bruising your face,
blurring your speech,
into that place
where abstraction becomes the noun
and absence adorns the verb.

Eighteenth Century Japanese Screen, Kyoto

I wish I could have told you

how the headrest of the couch
supporting my head comforted me,
or how the gold of the screen
blazed in the room like the new moon outside.
I loved these little people leaving,

a whole town of them—
I was the first person to understand this holocaust,
a whole town of the evacuated, here painted.

For a long time I saw the figures as fixed, art,
symbolic—
but now I see that they are moving,
all leaving even as they stand there
motionless and mute
before leaving the gold of paradise.

They are moving out, the living,
in evacuation to the hills, refugees
about to be exiled elsewhere.
In real life one and by one, usually, they go,
but here they are all poised together on the brink,

and since it's a hundred years later
they all are gone now anyway,
(they might have all gone at once in the holocaust of a war,
earthquake or tsunami—
the gold just a setting, with animals)

the progression, constantly moving forward
to the end of the horizon at the end of every edge
of every landscape and the edge of every town.

The gold is a convention and represents time and timelessness, you said,
but that's in my poem too, I said—
all these anonymous people,
their lives erupting from inside a curve in the landscape
like pines
the realm of gold sitting between the towns and white horses of here
and the *there* of eternity.

Doll's House

The music comes on with the lights,
the little opera of emptiness begins, the little
dance of no one there, just the rooms exhibited,
furniture in them like ideas,
a stage set waiting for action to come in out of the blue,
anything—a flute, or hopefully a whole orchestra waiting around
    the corner,
a little whirlwind of music that will trawl through the empty air.

But no,
even the little fire in the hearth is neon, warms no one,
the drawers in the painted chests
are filled with nothing, the tables
loaded with miniature, fake, repasts.
It's night outside, about to snow,
the dollhouse lights are on: from inside the big house
you see it like a thief,
pilfer its pockets,
wafted over by smells of cooking, and silence.

Inside the dark
a flute starts to play, imaginary people come in at the door:
invited to stay, they take off their coats,
tea is made in a miniature pot filled with water that hasn't boiled
    but tastes hot—oh,
it's good I hear you say, let's have crumpets too, and we put them
    on,
you and I, tiny, tiny, they're almost crumbs but we toast them,
and what kind of jam do you want, I say, on top of the butter,
and you say raspberry, reader,
and I give it to you.

I give it to you and we both eat it.
Outside the big house it's snowing.

Applied frost creeps up the sides of the doll house windows,
the fake fireplace glows electric,
our toy dog sleeps on the rug,
a hush falls over into this small house inside the big house,
we sleep in it—
I sleep, you sleep, he sleeps, she sleeps...
it sleeps, the real,
a sleep so delicious, we can dream in it,
as in a delirium, without sound...

windows opening into windows,
shoes never walked in at the door
that we slip on.

objet trouvé:

"the three dimensions, slightly concave, were so exquisitely proportional the absence of the fourth was scarcely felt." – Samuel Beckett

Question, Always the Same

The chair across from you gives off whispers
of the many who have left it,
an absence like a tide going out—
returning with little noises, sucking, spraying, lapping—
have you ever wanted what the sea retrieves with these sounds,
shells, bottles with messages,
fragments thought surely and forever lost?

Slipping into the fluid sprawlings of ink in a bottle on that beach,
the ambling undulations of those waves,
their liquid glance,
have you ever wanted
to slip and fall into such a message,
reclaim the very look of absence inside the blackness of that ink?

Have you ever wanted to go to sleep and write about it,
slip into the ocean and remember it,
slip and fall into it so you think you'll never come back, yet live—
have you ever wanted what you didn't know how to want,
what you didn't know how to get,
what you didn't know how to want yet?

Invalid Song

Walking with crutches
the afternoon
arrives on one foot
in the waters of evening.

Voices combing the anteroom
tangle on a pillow, the foot
ends propped up against a window,
its desire to move removed.

Very black, the perfume worn here,
absent as anesthetized pain,
moonlight seeping
over a dark floor.

Something climbs a carpet,
padding, restless.
The place it was looking for
whimpers in your sleep.

The foot says this is just like living—
the doctor's last word,
the drug's first image—
everyone pretending you have a choice.

Spring, a Triplet

I. *Driving Through Easter*

. . . the hills soft, velvet,
tunneled-through,
remembrance

life is
the ghost of the hills

you have to put it against time
to understand it:
put a space between them—
and you get . . .
nowhere

II. *Landscape*

in it are little chinks
like a cash register
opening,

every little jag up the hill
and then down,
sounds the same—

you're dying
all along the way

III. *Escarpment*

it's a cancer
sculpting out the land,
morphine in place,
body already missing—

most places I pass through I think
I wouldn't want to stop here,
belong—
my own life so weighted with meaning,

I wonder where are my wings?

VI. Green Box Large Glass

"The duality of the large glass: down below, the world of here and now; up there, the world of real reality, essences, and ideals. . . . The world up there is not the projection of our desires; we are their projection. Our desire is nostalgia, the remembrance of that world."

– Octavio Paz

"Delay, preserved chance: the bride, the bachelors and by implication the onlooker as well are suspended in a state of permanent desire."

– Calvin Tomkins

Desire

I've always wanted to understand desire.

Is it like a tree bent backwards, halfway
to the ground, drawn toward something
none of the other trees see?

Is *why* you desire *whatever* you desire
like what the *Tao Te Ching* defines
as the image of nothingness—
meet it and you do not see its face,
follow it and you do not see its back—

how can what's so elusive
keep obsessively reproducing itself
in so many ways?

Is desire itself
more desirable than the thing that lies
beyond it?

As if it wanted to say to you,
wanting anything

is already the baker's dozen,
where the thirteenth thing

gives you what you never wanted
that you never asked for
and supposedly desired.

The Bride (after Duchamp's *Large Glass*)

How willfully she manipulates desire
in order to arrange the wedding.

Whatever she does, she
foregoes the pleasure she does not desire
for the desire she desires.

The bachelors are her imaginary brothers,
contraptions for delay,
nine facets of the everyday,
connections that can wait
while they grow a distance
which is somehow far.

She's up there,
too anorexic to breed,
the idea of an idea;
her back to you, she beckons,
a finger, a carrot,
in a frame of her own
which you can never breach—

she herself is the event,
the wedding infra-thin,
the dress important.

objet trouvé:

"I give up my breath to the air." – John Keats

VII. Breather

"I spend my time very easily
but wouldn't know how to tell you
what I do . . . I'm a *respirateur*—
a breather."

– Marcel Duchamp

objet trouvé:

Lord: *"What is your studio?"*

Giacometti: *"Two feet that walk."*

Breath

Birds vocalize
even when you don't hear them,
and then you do
and they bring you back here
where a stone statue of a boy on a dolphin,
bereft of light, exists anyway.
Even in the dark he shines, still warm,
or in winter, cold as zero.
Even after the slivering or sharding of entropy,
even after an earthquake,
a tidal wave, Vesuvius,
there might still be parts of him
someone like yourself could glue together.

Whereas *you,*
you will become a space a body once fit:

breath
is not where staying is.
Breath, savagely arriving and leaving,
is absence incarnate,
the part of you that cannot be salvaged.
No pieces of it surface.
Breath *is*
nothing
as the boy on the dolphin hides what he knows—
that you come home without yourself,
somebody else will have to live *for* you.
(Something else sing
while the bird flies.)

Breather

For my father.

I.

Back in the time when you breathed
I would say breath to you and you
would answer back,
I would say breathe to you and you would do it:
I could have filled a community of breathers
with what you had,
it was free, a birthright,
day and night, black and white,
it was yours, given,
the acceptable inevitable companionship of opposites,
in and out, breath or death, breathe or die,
the human situation.

Birds talk about it
from one tree to another,
conversing across a small valley,
they know what they talk about,
they know something is wrong—
your breathing, or dying,
they know and talk about it,
while inside this room with big picture windows
we whisper about it.

We whisper
and they discuss it through trees
and across a small valley
in their secret language,
they chatter it all out, gossip,

how we lost our power:
what we couldn't imagine, couldn't control,
happened—

they trill it,
they chatter this shattering memory of you
as a breather.

II.

When you stopped doing it,
something happened.

Outside the windows
beside your bed
a huge flock of black birds appeared.
They started surging,
the minute you stopped doing it,
toward the windows,
sucked toward them in a vortex—
their small black bodies, more and more of them,
swirling into a presence outside the glass,
gyring up against it
until the faint dawn outside darkened with them.

Black flocks of night:
we watched speechless.

Then slowly,
gradually,
they ebbed away;
yes, they appeared,
out of nowhere
then vanished

like breath.

Friend to Man

Dog, snout rested on the edge of the couch,
your heart beating so fast I can feel it on my thigh,
(just because outside it's lightning),
old friend, who sleeps next to me,
follows me from room to room like a believer,
dog all day my only companion,
I would like to ask you—beyond loyalty,
what do you do for love?

Breather,
brother,
though covered thickly with a coat of fur,
your nose pointing up against the room's horizon,
I think you want not love,
but protection.
The protection of Indian music
hiding the thunder that accompanies lightning.

My little rug with a heart inside it,
my little rolled-up carpet of fear,
your terror of light in the night
is just being alive,
that skittering we hear
of fingers on the tabla,
is just being alive.

That crying of the strings,
the repetition that hides thunder,
the little beat that never strays but beats faster
when the sky lights up and exposes
a landscape with teeth,

the malice in that glance,
the sleeper inside your house,

death already inside the body,
is equal to being alive.

Horse-Washing Waterfall, Hokusai

Everything curves,
sagging around contours
like fall falling over the year, twilight over the day—
and, looking at the picture, you arrive at that moment, in autumn, at
    evening
where the year converges with twilight
and you see they are elements of the same thing,
time,

you see that it's there
where the tinge of color deepens the day into nothing,
it's there where the ache of blue becomes severest black—
there where the blue turns into a smoke you breathe and forget,
and it's in *the horse the two men the nestle of greenery the water streaming*
    behind them,
it's that moment, this second—
spirit sifting, drifting into form...

after you turn away from it,
the picture turns away from itself.
The men walk the horse home,
put it in a pasture near the hut they live in,
make tea, watch the evening
drift over what's left of the day.

The men, washing dishes,
are drawn over the waterfall, refreshed in the water, inundated by life,
their every moment superceded by the last,
their everything vanquished by the next thing,
the meaning of being is time.

The artist too has turned away.
He puts away his tools, cooks dinner,
the boiling noodles roil into waterfall.

Wings scissor the light,
dust fogs the road,
trees guzzle the wind,

tomorrow his brush
will make footprints
in paint that looks like snow.

Modern Fragment

I Have Another Name for You She Said

I see how inner
leads to other

from there
I can go anywhere

. . . everywhere waits

the place where I was
having disappeared now

this is where you receive me...

where all the nothing
in the world resides

. . . *what is the other name you have for me,*
I asked her,

your name is *then*

here in this empty
sleep

VIII. It's Always Everybody Else Who Dies.

"Buried with other members of Duchamp family
at the Cimetiere Monumental at Rouen. At his request,
his gravestone bears the inscription
'*D'ailleurs, c'est toujours les autres qui meurent.*'"

– Octavio Paz

Readymade: Of Velasquez

"I would start from as far away as possible,
when the illusion was complete, and come gradually nearer,
until suddenly what had been a hand, and a ribbon and a piece of velvet
dissolved into a fricassee of beautiful brushstrokes.
I thought I might learn something if I could catch the moment at which this
    transformation took place,
but it proved to be as elusive as the moment between sleeping and waking,

the fertile gap between art and living . . . "

Arrival

From your seat near the wings
you see the airplane's shadow,
a cross trailing your flight,
trawling small squares of fertility
and oceans of sand-colored land.

Up here you are fallow,
full of days like a vacation,
eating peanuts, leaving lipstick on a glass,
viewing from the air for two intangible hours
something as vaporous as clouds
stuck by something as obscure as shadow
to the ground.

In no time,
out of the blue,
we'll be,
a bodiless voice announces,
on the ground shortly.

Standing in the aisle you perspire
over your carry-on luggage,
impatient to arrive and pound the ground with useful feet,
led by emotions,
the way smells lead a dog toward bones.

In an ocean of light
your body meets its shadow.
A taxi pulls up,
the world slides in beside you—
your destination,
the consolation of pleasure,
and, led by emotions, you discover

arrival is the same as being
anywhere—
a town in which
a woman disappears
into a doorway of green
just getting the mail.

Looking at a Picture During Rain

Objects float in the room hanging on the wall,
and I know the subject of the painting is myself,

windows in that room are pictures,
plaster surfaces craze with their own history,

inside, a sleeper,
trying to breathe through to another world:

outside, a small lake of rain—
a fragment of this world trapped in a puddle,

a whole lake you could call it,
a memory of rain, a mercury of sky.

Living is an artist—
always creating

out of nothing,
reflections, form, liquid rules—

until the inside of life
turns into the outside,

as the living take a bath
in which they drown.

What Opens

Some of this music you listen to,
it shows people singing themselves,
their there-ness:
the rumble of rumba,
the sheer cliff of tango,
the rage of the inner cities—.
they shimmer up the walls of your house,
they visit the room of your head.

Outside it's getting dark,
that orchestra's about to begin:
the statue takes one step forward,
and puts his horn to his lips
as the trees wave you out,
or in—

you turn the light on
and what you see in the window
now
is yourself.
Foot resting on a couch,
you're about to say something.
So is the agapanthus beside you.

Buds appear
from inside its green leaves
like a secret,
sheathing the thrilling color to come—
what opens.

What opens,
opens into difference.
Closes for no reason.
This music too will have its head.

The Persian Boy

*"Then to the time of the chanty-men, with the light still cool and grey
on the road waters, we went downstream."*
– Mary Renault

Air is a river, dust is, and flesh.
We swim where we may, surrounded
by flowers, clouds, the dirt of earth.
We hear what music it makes,
existing as everything does, but *as* flesh.
I couldn't remember another life, even if anything beyond
this life existed.
I could not know more than this,
to be human and imagine the rest;
all I have is here, surrounds me—
I love a minor chord;
a sad note in the midst of splendor;
is that not what we have *here*,
is that not what *this* is.
Nothing ever changes because everything does, eons float over
existence, fingernails and hair grow
in tombs, many have
died before us.

objet trouvé:

"I did a coffee grinder which I made to explode; the coffee is tumbling down beside it; the gear wheels are above, and the knob is seen simultaneously at several points in its circuit, with an arrow to indicate movement. Without knowing it, I had opened a window onto something else." – Marcel Duchamp

Morandi, Still Life with Coffeepot

The coffeepot, only its tired lid and double-curved spout showing,
is a camel.
The more you look into the picture the more you want to—
the secret of everything is what every *thing* also is
(besides itself):

a cylinder with a lid casts a shadow
                    which is a man,
something broken,
                    or else a bone on the table,
the oval inside a handle   *a window.*

There are many windows:
the square lid of a canister seen at ¾ angle,
gleams of light that you can see through into a kind of atmosphere,

arches between things that become
                    other things,
between the pitcher and a candlestick,
                    ghostly background vases.

And what an odd assortment of things, and how many of them there are,
the table is full of them: slipshod, worn,
the used objects of everyday;

one form at least, (it's hard to tell)
                    is hanging off the edge of the table, and at the back, another,
if it is real, would be.

And then, the landscapes—
an inner life inside the still life
(inside the city, the bottled city):

nothing looks in the same direction,

the light is coming from another world

. . . one hole leads into a doorway,
one window into another . . .

What the Evening Knew

Books read, syllables adrift,
the children had been cricketed
to sleep by the one voice louder
and more insistent than theirs.
And finally, the composition fixed,
the rooms became the view,

and I knew
that of all there was,
in the midst of blue delphinium failing
to find a place for all their seeds,
this deep quiet
bothered by an outside murmur
was a quilt
that covered us in a protection.

I saw that what we long for
surrounds us
and is what we seek,
as if what we sought *were*
what is precious—
and who are we, miniscule and pulsing,
how could we dare
to say that it is not?

If I could paint this,
tomatoes, blue bowl, red table,
everything enveloped in the evening,
these fruits of life pounding like waves
in a sea, if I could paint
this redness in this blue
giving off a radiance
like dust in the night's light,
would that say more than the evening does—

locking all this in the eye
until the light was like a pulsar's
meaning get to know me,
I am what you are?

An afternoon was in the bowl,
you were the dust of it . . .
this is what the evening said it knew
and I believe it, don't you?

Notes on the Section Headings and Poems

Home: the present state of existence; Home: the grave. A house is the only recurring symbol of the human body in dreams, Freud.

"I thought I might be happier after dinner, but I have had dinner." Florine Stett-hiemer: "I am very unhappy—and I don't think I deserve to be," she wrote in her diary after hanging a show of her work. "I thought I might be happier after dinner—but I have had dinner." *Marcel Duchamp*, a biography by Calvin Tomkins p. *173*

The word readymades here are from the notebooks of Ioanna Carlsen; their titles, assisted by Marcel Duchamp.

"Readymade: With Hidden Noise": Quotations are Marcel Duchamp's; the last stanza is Francis Naumann from *The Trickster* by Lewis Hyde.

"Readymade: Traveller's Folding Item": Quotations are from Emerson, James Lord, a documentary on the Sahara.

"Readymade: A Country Road. A Tree. Evening": Quotations are from Samuel Beckett and from books on Beckett.

"Readymade: Why Not Sneeze?": Quotations are from Samuel Beckett, Alberto Giacometti, George Balanchine.

"Readymade: Of Velasquez": Quotations are from Kenneth Clark, Robert Rauschenberg.

"The Bride": "Again and again in Duchamp's notes, [in The Green Box] there is a joyous sense of a mind that has broken free of all restraints—a mind at play in a game of its own devising, whose resolution is infinitely delayed. . . . The bride . . . is like Keats's maiden on the Grecian urn, forever in passage between desire and fulfillment, . . . The bride, the bachelors, and by implication the onlooker as well are suspended in a state of permanent desire." – Calvin Tomkins

The Large Glass: "Duchamp's painting is a transparent glass; as a genuine monument it is inseparable from the place it occupies and the space that surround it; it is an incomplete painting that is perpetually completing itself. Because it is an image that reflects the image of whoever contemplates it, we are never able to look at it without seeing ourselves." . . . "*The Large Glass* . . . is a version of the ancient myth of the great Goddess, Virgin, Mother, Giver and Exterminator of life. It is not a modern myth: it is the modern version—or vision—of the Myth." – Octavio Paz

"I Wanted to Fall": "*the wet path opens*" is from Karl Kerenyi, *Hermes, Guide of Souls.* "The wet path" is the ancient Greek metaphor for the sea, and in a way, life.

"Breather": The image is from *Greek Religion* by Marin P. Nilsson: ". . . the rapid arrival or disappearance of a god is often compared to the flight of a bird."

"*D'ailleurs, c'est toujours les autres qui meurent.*" Epitaph for Marcel Duchamp ("It's always everybody else who dies"); written by the artist for his own tombstone and quoted later by Octavio Paz in *Appearance Stripped Bare.*

Ioanna Carlsen's poems and stories have appeared in *Agni, Poetry, Field, Alaska Quarterly Review, Hudson Review, Prairie Schooner, Ploughshares, Beloit Poetry Journal, Poetry Daily,* and *Glimmer Train,* among others. In 2002, she won the Glimmer Train Poetry Open, and in 2015, her collection *The Whisperer* won second place in the New Mexico Press Women's Book Contest. Five of her poems also appear in *Pomegranate Seeds,* an anthology of Greek-American Poetry.